Theodore Roosevelt

BY XINA M. UHL

Published by The Child's World®
1980 Lookout Drive • Mankato, MN 56003-1705
800-599-READ • www.childsworld.com

Acknowledgments
The Child's World®: Mary Swensen, Publishing Director
Red Line Editorial: Editorial direction and production
The Design Lab: Design

Photographs ©: GraphicaArtis/Corbis, cover, 1; Corbis,
4; Underwood & Underwood/Library of Congress, 7;
Everett Historical/Shutterstock Images, 8, 15; AS400 DB/
Corbis, 11; George Prince/Library of Congress, 12; Detroit
Publishing Company/Library of Congress, 16; Gary Tognoni/
iStockphoto, 19; Harris & Ewing, Inc./Corbis, 21

ISBN 9781503808768
LCCN 2015958435

Printed in the United States of America
Mankato, MN
June, 2016
PA02303

ABOUT THE AUTHOR

Xina M. Uhl loves history, hiking, travel, and pizza. She lives in southern California with her family and a bunch of dogs.

Table of Contents

President McKinley was visiting an exposition just before he was killed.

CHAPTER ONE

Two Presidents

It was September 6, 1901. Many people had come to Buffalo, New York. They were there for an **exposition**. President William McKinley greeted them. A man in the crowd came forward. He had a cloth on one hand. McKinley reached out to shake his other hand. The cloth fell away. It had been hiding a gun. The man shot McKinley two times.

The vice president heard the bad news. His name was Theodore Roosevelt. He was in Vermont at Lake Champlain. He rushed to see McKinley.

The president had been shot in the chest and **abdomen**. But doctors said he would get better.

So Roosevelt left. He joined his family in the Adirondack Mountains. They hiked up Mount Marcy. It is the tallest mountain in New York. There, he got two **telegrams**. They each had news about the president. One said that he was getting worse. The other said that he was dying. Roosevelt hurried to the train station. His secretary met him there with a third telegram. This one said that McKinley had died.

Now, Roosevelt was president of the United States. He was 42 years old. He was the youngest person ever to become president. He loved to work hard. He had a lot of energy. He also had many new ideas. His time as president would change the job forever.

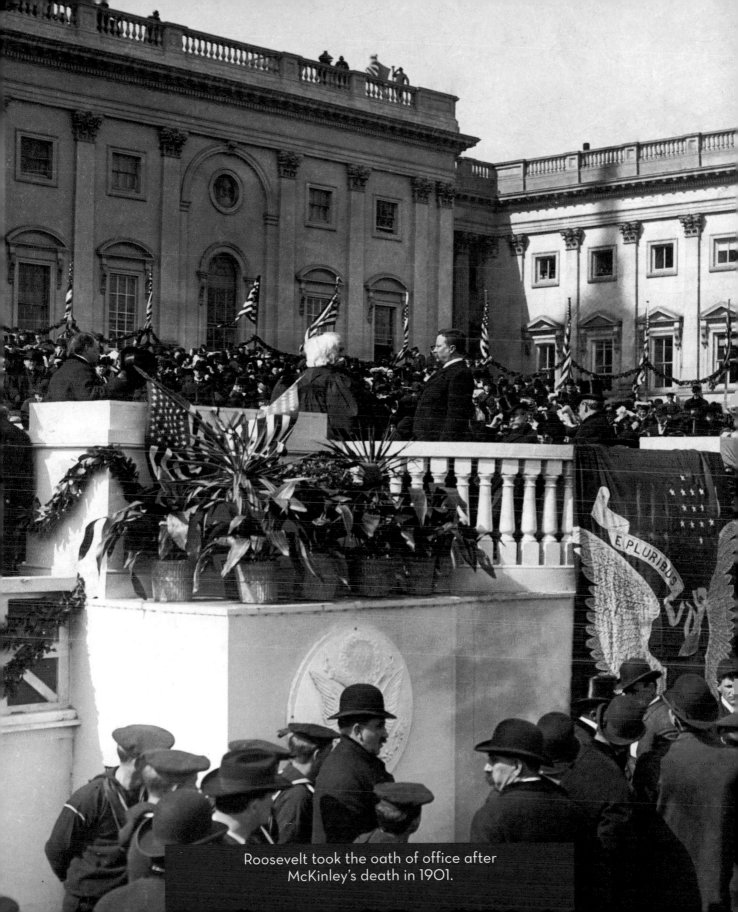

Roosevelt took the oath of office after McKinley's death in 1901.

Roosevelt (lower left) grew up in a wealthy home.

CHAPTER TWO

Mind and Body

Theodore Roosevelt was born on October 27, 1858. He lived in New York City. His parents were wealthy. They had four children. Private **tutors** taught Roosevelt at home. His mother also helped to teach him.

Roosevelt had **asthma** as a child. But he stayed active. He read. He loved to study nature. He examined animals such as mice and fish. He was smart and curious. But he was not strong. His father said, "You have the mind, but you have not the body. . . . You must make your body."

Roosevelt listened to his father. Roosevelt exercised a lot. He swam. He rode horses. He hiked. He grew strong. He called it "the **strenuous** life." Over time, his asthma improved.

In 1876, he went to Harvard University. He studied German and writing. He learned to box. He also met a woman named Alice Lee. He began to **court** her. In October 1880, they got married. Then, he went to Columbia Law School. Law school bored him. So he wrote a book about the War of 1812.

He quit school the next year. He joined the New York State Assembly. It made laws for New York. He was there from 1882 to 1884. He helped the state. Powerful people controlled the government. They were called **bosses**. They chose who got government jobs. Bosses picked people who would help them. Those people did not always help the state.

Roosevelt spent time in the West after his wife Alice died.

Roosevelt wanted **reform**. The Republican **Party** bosses did not like this. They wanted to stay in power.

In 1884, his first child, Alice, was born. It was February 12, 1884. Two days later, his wife died. She had a kidney disease. His mother died on the same day. She had typhoid fever. Roosevelt left New York. The Dakota Badlands offered him a place to grieve. He bought two ranches and kept cattle. He hunted. He stayed there for two years.

Edith Carow and Roosevelt had known
each other since they were young.

CHAPTER THREE

From Cattle Rancher to President

★ ★ ★

In 1886, Roosevelt came home to New York. His cattle had died. Drought and blizzards had killed them. He was also lonely. That year, he married Edith Carow. They had known each other since they were young. They would go on to have five children together.

Roosevelt ran for mayor of New York City in 1886. He lost. Over the next ten years, he wrote six books. He wrote about the West. He wrote about hunting and ranching.

Roosevelt held many jobs. He worked for the police board in 1895. He became an assistant secretary of the navy in 1897. In 1898, war broke out with Spain. The United States wanted to free Cuba from Spanish rule. Roosevelt joined the fight. He led a **cavalry** in Cuba. They were called Rough Riders. They fought hard. Roosevelt became a war hero. He ran for **governor** of New York in 1899. He won later that year.

But Roosevelt made the Republican Party bosses unhappy. They wanted people they liked to work for New York. They usually got their way. But Roosevelt wanted people who were good at those jobs to work there. The bosses took action. They made sure he would become vice president. They thought he would

Roosevelt (center) gained popularity as leader of the Rough Riders.

not have power. The president would listen to the
bosses. Roosevelt would not be able to make changes.

Roosevelt became vice president in 1901. But
that year, President William McKinley was killed.
Roosevelt was now president. And the bosses could
not control him.

Roosevelt kept large companies like
J. P. Morgan under control.

CHAPTER FOUR

At Home and across the Ocean

Before Roosevelt, presidents did not have much power. Party bosses and companies had a lot of power. They had the most money. They told presidents what to do. Roosevelt changed that.

Some big companies put small companies out of business. Others treated workers poorly. Roosevelt wanted companies to be fair. Congress helped him. They made laws. The laws kept big companies from having too much power. That way smaller companies could compete. And more workers were treated fairly.

Roosevelt loved nature. He wanted to keep it safe. He turned 125 million acres (505,800 sq km) into national forests. It almost tripled the U.S. national park land. In the national parks, water was kept clean. He also made areas where birds' homes were kept safe.

Roosevelt also helped to build a canal. It would make traveling from the East Coast to the West Coast faster. Ships used to sail around South America. Roosevelt wanted a canal through Panama. It was in Central America. Colombia owned the land. They said no. So Roosevelt helped Panama separate from Colombia. It became a new country in 1903. Now America could dig the canal. It was called the Panama Canal.

Roosevelt added land to Yosemite National Park and other national parks.

In 1904, Roosevelt ran for another term as president. This time, he wanted to win on his own. He won easily. And he had a message for the world. He would "speak softly and carry a big stick." This meant he would talk before fighting. But he would also show the country was strong. He added ships to the U.S. Navy.

Roosevelt's time as president ended in 1909. He helped William Taft run for president. He thought Taft would continue to reform. Taft won. But he did not do what Roosevelt wanted. So Roosevelt started the Bull Moose Party. It would support reform. He ran for president again in 1912. He lost.

World War I started in 1914. Roosevelt's son Quentin fought. He was killed in 1918. Roosevelt was very sad. He died from a blood clot the next year.

Roosevelt changed the American government. He gave the president's job power. He made it different for every president after him.

Roosevelt (left) helped William Taft run for president.

TIMELINE

1850

← **October 27, 1858** Theodore Roosevelt is born in New York City.

← **September 1876** Roosevelt begins his education at Harvard University.

← **October 27, 1880** Roosevelt marries Alice Lee.

← **December 1880** Roosevelt enters Columbia Law School.

← **1882** Roosevelt joins the New York State Assembly.

← **February 14, 1884** Roosevelt's wife Alice and his mother die on the same day.

← **June 9, 1884** Roosevelt leaves to live in the Dakota Badlands.

← **December 2, 1886** Roosevelt marries Edith Carow.

← **May 6, 1895** Roosevelt is elected president of the Board of Police Commissioners.

← **April 19, 1897** Roosevelt is appointed Assistant Secretary of the navy.

← **November 8, 1898** Roosevelt is elected governor of the state of New York.

← **November 6, 1900** Roosevelt is elected vice president.

← **September 14, 1901** Roosevelt becomes the 26th president of the United States.

← **1904** Roosevelt is reelected to the presidency.

← **March 1909** Roosevelt's presidency ends.

← **July 14, 1918** Roosevelt's son Quentin is killed in World War I.

← **January 6, 1919** Roosevelt dies.

1920

abdomen (AB-do-men) The body between the chest and hips is called the abdomen. President McKinley was shot in the chest and the abdomen.

asthma (AZ-muh) Asthma makes it hard to breathe and causes sufferers to cough and wheeze. Roosevelt had severe asthma as a child.

bosses (BOSS-is) Leaders in political parties who control votes are called bosses. Roosevelt's reform ideas made Republican Party bosses angry.

cavalry (KAV-ul-ree) Soldiers who fight while riding horses are called cavalry. The Rough Riders cavalry fought in the Spanish-American War.

court (KORT) To court someone is to try to gain someone else's love with the intent of marriage. Roosevelt began to court Alice Lee.

exposition (eks-pe-ZI-shun) An exposition is a public display of objects. McKinley greeted people at an exposition.

governor (GUV-uh-ner) A governor is the head of a state or colony. Roosevelt was governor of New York.

party (PAR-tee) A group of people with similar beliefs who try to get elected is called a party. Roosevelt was part of the Republican Party.

reform (ri-FORM) When someone makes something better, they reform it. Roosevelt wanted to reform the New York government.

strenuous (STREN-yu-uhss) Something that is strenuous is very active. Roosevelt believed in "the strenuous life."

telegrams (TEL-e-grams) Telegrams are messages sent using a telegraph. Roosevelt got three telegrams; the last one told of McKinley's death.

tutors (TOO-torz) People who teach subjects outside of school are tutors. Roosevelt had private tutors as a child.

In the Library

Burgan, Michael. *Who Was Theodore Roosevelt?*
New York: Grosset & Dunlap, 2014.

Rappaport, Doreen. *To Dare Mighty Things: The Life of Theodore Roosevelt.* New York: Disney Hyperion, 2013.

Rosenstock, Barb. *The Camping Trip that Changed America.*
New York: Dial Books for Young Readers, 2012.

On the Web

Visit our Web site for links about Theodore Roosevelt:
childsworld.com/links

Note to Parents, Teachers, and Librarians: We routinely verify our Web links to make sure they are safe and active sites. So encourage your readers to check them out!

INDEX